to Marion

to love —

to life —

to us —

Bob

Here's

Writings and Photograph

to Life!

hat Express the Joy and Beauty of Being

Selected by Aileene Herrbach Neighbors

Designed by Eva Sue Szela

♛

Hallmark Crown Editions

PHOTOGRAPHS: Jacqueline Casey, pages 46-47, dust jacket back; Dr. E. R. Degginger, pages 34-35; Phoebe Dunn, pages 32-33; Sally Ehrlich, pages 36-37; Free Lance Photographers Guild, Inc., pages 54-55; Paul Fusco, pages 6-7, 12, 13, 14, 18, 24-25, 50-51, 60-61; Harv Gariety, pages 40, 41, title page; James B. Gross, pages 16-17; Don James (Louis Mercier), pages 30-31; Jack Kenward, pages 8-9; Elyse Lewin, page 5; Robert Llewelyn, page 52; Tom Myers, page 29; Linda Neils, page 38; Larry Nicholson, pages 44-45, 56-57; Kosti Ruohomaa (Black Star), page 58; Robert Segura, pages 48, 49; Tomas Sennett, pages 20-21; Walter Shostal, page 42; Edward Simpson, pages 4-5, 22; Paul Slaughter (Art Expo), page 11; Otto Storch, dust jacket front; Dr. John C. Weaver, page 16; Sam Zarember, pages 26-27.

ACKNOWLEDGMENTS: Excerpt from *The Second Treasury of Kahlil Gibran* by Kahlil Gibran. Copyright © 1962 by The Citadel Press, Inc. Reprinted by permission. Excerpts by Terence Cardinal Cooke, Michael E. DeBakey, Walter Cronkite and Joan Baez from *Look* Magazine (July 27, 1971) and an excerpt by William Hedgepeth from *Look* Magazine (January 12, 1971) reprinted by permission of Cowles Communications, Inc. Copyright © Cowles Communications, Inc. 1971. Excerpt by the Reverend Billy Graham from *Family Circle* (April 1972) reprinted by permission of Mr. Fred Dienert. Excerpt from page 214 in *I'm OK — You're OK* by Thomas A. Harris. Copyright © 1967, 1968, 1969 by Thomas A. Harris, M.D. Reprinted by permission of Harper & Row, Publishers, Inc. "Daylight" by a Pawnee Indian from *My Poetry Book* selected and arranged by Grace Thompson Huffard and Laura Carlisle. Published by Holt, Rinehart and Winston, Inc. Excerpt by Yael Dayan from "The Good Life" in *McCall's* Magazine reprinted by permission of International Famous Agency. Copyright © 1970 by Yael Dayan. Excerpt reprinted from *To My Daughters, With Love* by Pearl S. Buck by permission of The John Day Company, Inc., publisher. Copyright 1949, 1957, 1960, 1962, 1963, 1964 by Pearl S. Buck. Copyright 1967 by Pearl S. Buck Foundation Inc. "The Happy Mood" by Florence Jacobs. © 1964, Florence B. Jacobs. Excerpt by Eda LeShan from *Woman's Day* Magazine (November 1970). Reprinted by permission of Eda LeShan and Ann Elmo Agency, Inc. "Perfect Moments" from the book *Stillmeadow Daybook* by Gladys Taber. Copyright © 1955 by Gladys Taber. Reprinted by permission of J. B. Lippincott Company. Excerpt from *Fireflies* by Rabindranath Tagore. Copyright 1928 by Macmillan Publishing Co., Inc., renewed 1955 by Rathindranath Tagore. Reprinted with permission of Macmillan Publishing Co., Inc., the Trustees of the Tagore Estate and Macmillan, London and Basingstoke. "Barter" reprinted with permission of Macmillan Publishing Co., Inc. from *Collected Poems* by Sara Teasdale. Copyright 1917 by Macmillan Publishing Co., Inc., renewed 1945 by Mamie T. Wheless. "Who Will Make the City Joyful?" from *Faces in the City* by James Kavanaugh, Copyright © 1972 by James Kavanaugh, published by Nash Publishing Corp., Los Angeles. Excerpt from *Markings*, by Dag Hammarskjöld, translated by Leif Sjoberg and W. H. Auden. Copyright © 1964 by Alfred A. Knopf, Inc. and Faber & Faber Ltd. Reprinted by permission of Alfred A. Knopf, Inc. and Faber & Faber Ltd. Excerpt from *Human Like Me, Jesus* by Malcolm Boyd. Copyright © 1971 by Malcolm Boyd. Reprinted by permission of Simon & Schuster, Inc.

Set in Trump Mediaeval.
Printed on Hallmark Crown Royale Book paper.

Here's to Life!

Barter

Life has loveliness to sell,
   All beautiful and splendid things,
Blue waves whitened on a cliff,
   Soaring fire that sways and sings,
And children's faces looking up
Holding wonder like a cup.

Life has loveliness to sell,
   Music like a curve of gold,
Scent of pine trees in the rain,
   Eyes that love you, arms that hold,
And for your spirit's still delight,
Holy thoughts that star the night.

Spend all you have for loveliness,
    Buy it and never count the cost;
For one white singing hour of peace
    Count many a year of strife well lost,
And for a breath of ecstasy
Give all you have been, or could be.

Sara Teasdale

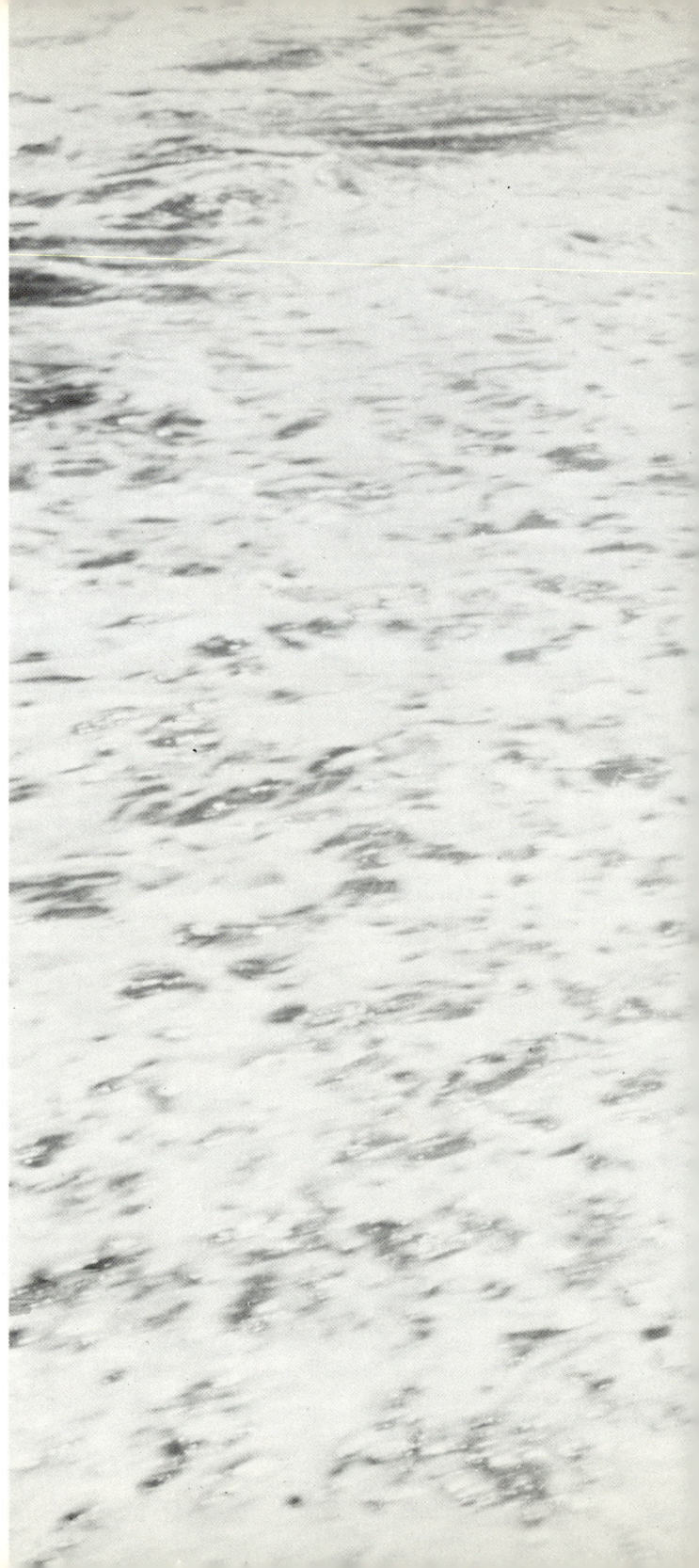

Bird born above the need for singing,
Born for soaring, dipping, swinging,
Wheeling out an arc of sky
With your strange, triumphal cry…
Now brushing cloud, now skimming sea,
Brave gull, aloof and proudly free!
As you span the current's buoyant air,
My soul soars to meet you there!

Mary R. Hurley

6

Happy times and bygone days are never lost....
In truth, they grow more wonderful within the heart that keeps them.

Kay Andrew

The Happy Mood

It's lovely, and it's *mine,*
and I shall not expose it
to the wind, the weather
or the world's comments;
in a green-edged corner
of my heart I'll enclose it
with mist and moonbeams...
and it *needn't* make sense!

Florence Jacobs

The inky prophecies of today's newspaper
are gloomy, Lord....

   But I don't want to be dismayed
by what appears hard or even hopeless.
   I want to celebrate life.
   Blood flows through my veins.

Rain falls, Lord. Waters surge through the earth.
   I know that the sun is up, Lord,
even when it is hidden by low gray clouds.
   I know that the wind is here, even when it
is so still. Look! A leaf trembles on that tree.
   I can see yellows, reds, blues, greens,
black and white.

Love. It is all around me. Sometimes
it is called hate.
  I feel like singing, smelling, looking,
biting, laughing, tasting, crying, painting,
walking, dancing, running…
  Living, Lord.

Malcolm Boyd

Time is...
Too slow for those who wait,
Too swift for those who fear,
Too long for those who grieve,
Too short for those who rejoice;
But for those who love,
Time is not.

Henry van Dyke

I live in a very small house,
but my windows look out on a very large world.
Confucius

For the heart that is free,
life is a celebration of beauty,
a festival of the spirit.

Ed Cunningham

...Leisure is a time for "recreation,"
a time to build up physical
and spiritual reserves.

Terence Cardinal Cooke

19

Hunger is my native place in the land
of the passions. Hunger for fellowship,
hunger for righteousness — for a fellowship
founded on righteousness, and a righteousness
attained in fellowship.

Only life can satisfy the demands of life.
And this hunger of mine can be satisfied
for the simple reason that the nature of life
is such that I can realize my individuality
by becoming a bridge for others, a stone
in the temple of righteousness.

Dag Hammarskjöld

...Oneness we have shared since creation,
that source of our common meaning.
Had creation been accidental,
then we would be without significance.
If substance came from nothingness,
then we would be nothing.
We would not still be in the midst of unfolding....

William Hedgepeth

Who Will Make
The City Joyful?

Who will make the city joyful
　Who will wipe away its tears?
Who will fill the streets with gladness
　Who will calm the old folks' fears?
Who will tell the children stories
　Who will make their clear eyes gleam?
Who will keep the men from killing
　Who will give the women dreams?

Maybe twenty thousand minstrels
　Twenty thousand poets' words
Maybe fifty thousand dancers
　Maybe clowns and talking birds
Flowers on all the city's corners
　Trees on all the city streets
Maybe fragrance from the sewers
　Sing-alongs in subway seats.

27

Maybe buses painted purple
  Maybe no more numbered days
Bells that ring in all the buildings
  Merchants learning how to play
Maybe parks for picnic lunches
  Waterfalls and bubbling streams
Maybe flowers on cold computers--
  Crowning IBM machines.

Maybe plumbers playing trumpets
  Salesmen strumming their guitars
Lawyers nursing tender flowers
  Businessmen exploring stars
Maybe potters, weavers, artists
  Craftsmen, architects who dare,
Maybe muralists and sculptors
  Maybe anyone who cares.

Maybe honest politicians
  Radicals with angry screams
Maybe socialists and Marxists
  Maybe silent men who dream
Maybe shoppers loving beggars
  Gently smiling flower maids
Those who listen to the children
  Those who still enjoy parades.

Who will sit among the flowers
  See the sun and sky above?
Who will make the city joyful
  Who will make us laugh and love?
Maybe mothers loving babies
  Maybe gentle eyes that see.
Or beyond the other maybes
  Maybe you and maybe me.

                    James Kavanaugh

Reality, for some people, is broader than it is for others, because they have looked more, lived more, read more, experienced more, and thought more.

Thomas A. Harris

Let us have life and peace, and the Good Life will follow.

Yael Dayan

For me, the solitude of the early morning
is the most precious time of the day—
and the only time that I have
to myself alone. There is a quiet serenity
that disappears a few hours later
with the hustle and bustle of the multitude
getting ready for work. The early
morning hours symbolize for me a rebirth;
the anxieties, frustrations and woes
of the preceding day seem to have been
washed away during the night. God has
granted another day of life. He has granted
another chance to do something good
and worthwhile for humanity.

Michael E. DeBakey

...I go to the sea by small boat.
   With one's vessel propelled by the same
   power of wind that moved the ancients,
   faced by the same challenges and beauty of nature,
   at work or unleashed, one can feel a kinship
   with all living things and achieve,
   at least momentarily, some degree of serenity.

   Walter Cronkite

Joy freed from the bond of earth's slumber
rushes into numberless leaves, and dances
in the air for a day.

Rabindranath Tagore

The appearance of things changes
according to the emotions, and thus we see magic
and beauty in them, while the magic and beauty
are really in ourselves.

Kahlil Gibran

I am often overcome with the concept of life as a river. A river that flows very fast. In that river is all the beauty, all the glory and, at the same time, all the agony and the pain that any of us has either dreamed of or experienced.

Joan Baez

Perfect Moments

There is always one moment in a day when I think my heart will break. Such a moment, I think, all women have, and men too, when all the meaning of life seems distilled and caught up and you feel you can never, never bear to leave it. It may be when you turn and look down a blazing autumn road, or it may be when you see your house under great ancient trees, or it may be in the city when you look up at a towering apartment building and see one light and think "that is mine." It may be any one of a number of things, according to the circumstances of your life.

But there is the moment when all the heartaches and sorrows of your life suddenly diminish and only the fine brave things stand out. You breathe sharp clean air, your eyes lift to the eternal wideness of the sky.

Anybody has moments like this to store up, but some people are too busy adding up their frustrations to appreciate them. And yet, all we need is an awareness of the beauty in life to make us richly content. My definition of happiness is just the ability to garner the perfect moments.

Gladys Taber

46

Life is very short....

The things you put a lot of time into
have very little permanent worth.
The permanent things are matters
of the spirit and of the heart.

Billy Graham

...The pursuit of art through some chosen form,
planned for and achieved by determination
and persistence, brings permanent contentment
and the illumination of genuine happiness
to the human spirit. Life is never dull, the creature is
never bored, when he — or she — becomes the creator.

Pearl S. Buck

L ife is the love that reaches out building bridges across gulfs of uncertainty...
to touch hands, hearts and souls in the experience of union.

Peter Seymour

Daylight

Day is here! Day is here, is here!
Arise, my son, lift thine eyes,
Day is here! Day is here, is here!
Day is here! Day is here, is here!
Look up, my son, and see the day.
Day is here! Day is here, is here!

Lo, the deer! Lo, the deer, the deer
Comes from her covert of the night!
Day is here! Day is here, is here!
Lo, the deer! Lo, the deer, the deer!
All creatures wake and see the light.
Day is here! Day is here, is here!
Day is here! Day is here, is here!

Pawnee Indian

56

The best thing about being human is our capacity
to be creative and spontaneous —
to change our minds, to be adventurers.

Eda LeShan